A POCKET GUIDE TO
ITALY

American Forces Information Service
Washington, D.C. • 1987

DoD PG-6B*
DA Pam 360-401 (Rev 1987)*
NAVPERS 15405-A (Rev 1987)*
AFP 2164 (Rev 1987)*
NAVMC 2690 (Rev 1987)*

CONTENTS

Welcome 3
Italy—A Profile 4
Why You Are Going 6
The Armed Forces 8
A Bit of History 9
Your Hosts—The Italians 11
A Word about Terrorism 16
Getting Around 17
You and the Law 20
Daily Living 23
You and Metric 27
Language Guide 30
Sights to See 35
Getting Ready To Go 38

*This pocket guide replaces DoD PG-6A/DA Pam 360401/NAVPERS 15405/AFP 216/NAVMC
2690, which should he used until supplies are exhausted

2

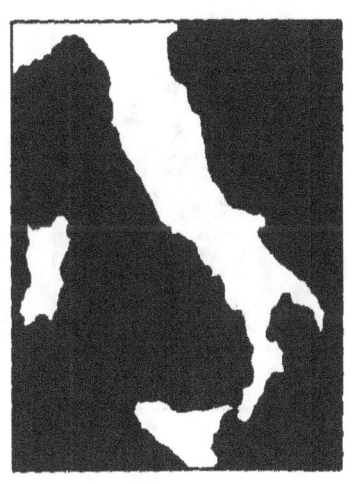

WELCOME TO ITALY

Your assignment to Italy is a good reason to start celebrating!

During your tour of duty in Italy, you will have more pleasant and interesting experiences than any tourist could ever afford.

You will be working and living side-by-side with Italian military members and civilians.

You will share their foods, the tourist sights that most Americans see only in travel books and, most of all, the people's friendliness.

You will be on an adventure that hundreds of thousands of tourists pay dearly to experience for a few days or weeks.

ITALY—A PROFILE

THE PEOPLE

Population: Estimated 60 million citizens, primarily Italian, with small groups of German-, French-, Slovene- and Albanian-Italians.

Literacy rate: Estimated 93 percent.

Per capita income: $3,040.

THE COUNTRY

Area: 116,303 square miles, about the size of Georgia and Florida combined.

Capital: Rome, with a population estimated at 2.6 million.

Other major cities: Milan, Naples, Florence, Venice, Turin.

Terrain: Mostly rugged and mountainous.

Climate: Generally mild.

THE GOVERNMENT

A republic, with a founding date of June 2, 1946.

Branches: Executive branch headed by a president (chief of state), a council of ministers (cabinet) headed by a president (prime minister). Legislative branch composed of 630-member Chamber of Deputies and 322-member Senate. Judicial branch consists of an independent constitutional court.

THE FLAG

Three vertical bands—green, white and red.

WHY YOU ARE GOING

As a member of the U.S. armed forces, you probably will be stationed in one of seven different parts of Italy.

If you are assigned to Allied Forces Southern Europe, one headquarters of the North Atlantic Treaty Organization, you will be living just outside the port city of Naples.

Many Navy men and women are stationed in that area, since elements of the U.S. Sixth Fleet are home-ported at Gaeta, some 60 miles north of Naples.

Other Navy facilities are located on Italy's largest islands. Sigonella Naval Air Facility is outside the city of Catania on the east coast of Sicily. La Maddalena, off the north coast of Sardinia, is the site of a U.S. Navy support activity.

The Southern European Task Force has its headquarters in Vicenza, just west of Venice, at the Army's Camp Ederle, a large, modern installation with an important mission.

And Aviano Air Base is a major Air Force installation about 50 miles north of Venice at the base of the Italian Alps.

Two other major Air Force installations in Italy are San Vito dei Normanni Air Station, located just outside the ancient Roman seaport of Brindisi, and Comiso Air Base, 30 miles southwest of Catania.

Close to Florence is the other Army installation, Camp Darby, located between the west coast cities of Livorno and Pisa.

All U.S. armed forces units in Italy maintain constant readiness as part of the United States' commitment to NATO.

THE ARMED FORCES

Approximately 600,000 men—there are no female service members—serve in all branches of Italy's armed forces. Army service of 12 months is required for every able-bodied male; if he signs up for the navy, his period of service will be 14 months.

The Carabinieri, the elite national police force, has about 90,000 members. They wear a distinctive uniform that makes them easy to find if you need help.

A BIT OF HISTORY

Italy has been a republic since 1946, when the monarchy was abolished in a national election and a constituent assembly was elected to draw up the plans for the present republic.

However, modern Italian history dates from 1870 with the unification of the entire peninsula under King Victor Emmanuel II of the House of Savoy.

From 1870 until 1922, Italy was a constitutional monarchy with a parliament elected under limited suffrage.

In 1922, Benito Mussolini came to power and, in the course of the next few years, eliminated the old political parties, curtailed liberties and installed a fascist dictatorship called the Corporate State.

The king, with little power, remained titular head of state.

After World War II, the constitution of I 948 abolished the monarchy and set up a republic with a two-chamber parliament, a separate judiciary and an executive branch.

The president, who is the head of state, is elected by the

parliament for a seven-year term.

The president nominates the prime minister from the parliament (which must vote to confirm the nomination), and that individual appoints the other ministers of the cabinet.

Both houses of the parliament—the 322-member Senate and the 630-member Chamber of Deputies—are elected for a maximum of five years, but either may be dissolved before the end of that term, and early elections may be called.

There is an independent constitutional court whose function is to determine the constitutionality of laws.

In addition to the central government and its organizations, there are 93 provinces and 20 regions with limited powers of self-government.

Whatever your role as a member of the armed forces is in Italy, remember that you are not in the country to comment on its politics or parties. Elections, candidates, parties—the entire process of voting—are the responsibility of Italian citizens, not American visitors.

YOUR HOSTS—THE ITALIANS

Even grade school geography students in the United States quickly recognize Italy.

It is a 700-mile long peninsula shaped like a boot extending into the heart of the Mediterranean.

That familiar landmark on the European map is home to about 60 million Italians who live in a total area only about half the size of Texas. Italy has the fifth highest population density in Europe—about 483 persons per square mile.

On the west and south it includes the large islands of Sardinia and Sicily, Pantelleria and the Eolian group.

Italy is very mountainous, with the Alps separating the country from the rest of Europe across its northern width and a spine formed by the Apennine range running down the middle of its 700-mile length.

Surrounded by five seas and with Sicily just 90 miles from mainland Africa, the Italian peninsula has been the jumping-off place to the African continent and to the far reaches of the Orient for centuries.

Besides the mountains, the main geographic areas are the lakes region along the northern border and the lush valleys in the northeast, which border the Po River at the start of its journey into the gulf of Venice.

The rich river valley harbors a good portion of the nation's agriculture and most of its industrial power.

To some foreign visitors, Italy is still "two countries"— north and south — although the rigid distinctions of the past are blurring.

The last fingers of the *autostrada* (highway) have now reached the bottom of the boot, and a vigorous promotion of the *Meridione,* as the region is called by the Italians, has been under way for some time to attract commercial and industrial development.

Italy is a nation and a people that gave the world two of its greatest periods of civilization—the Roman Empire and the Renaissance.

The Italians are guardians of riches that would take decades to be seen and appreciated. And they are happy and eager to share their good fortune with you, their American guest.

Because you will be in Italy for a longer period than most tourists, you will have opportunities to visit more than just a few major cities and sights in this fascinating land.

From your installation, you will have a base from which to make trips into all of the provinces of this highly regionalized country.

By enjoying the regional food specialties and native customs, you will discover sides of Italy little known to vacationers.

And through your work and daily living you will enjoy the Italians as personal friends, since the friendliness of the Italian people is legendary.

COURTESIES

As soon as you arrive in Italy, you will discover that your hosts love to live life to the fullest.

Even when times are not the best, they have a smile for the world.

On the streets and highways, they drive with abandon, whipping their cars and motorcycles in and out of traffic.

When they meet on the streets or in houses or cafes, hugs, kisses on the cheeks and handshakes are given freely.

But most of all, they have a zest for life and love to talk.

In their conversation with each other, you will see the Italian way of life at its best.

Everyone has a view on everything and expresses it with vigor.

There is more talking than there is listening, but all enjoy the sport of conversation.

A small traffic accident will rapidly bring together a crowd, and each spectator will have a view to give to the policeman who soon arrives to investigate.

You're a guest in the country, so take the first step early in your tour and start learning the language. As you do, an entirely new view of the Italians and their way of life will open to you.

Just don't start discussing politics or other sensitive subjects. Italians give their opinions and criticisms freely, but love their country deeply.

Any attempt you make at speaking Italian will be warmly received. You'll be corrected in your pronunciation by your hosts, but that's the easy way to learn a foreign language.

At the same time, you will find that Italians are very interested in you personally. In the course of your conversations, you will be asked what may seem to you to be extremely personal questions regarding your life, your family and the rent you pay. These are subjects that Italians discuss among themselves, so they are not being rude when they ask you the same questions.

If you are embarrassed by a question, say so. This is acceptable since frankness is another facet of the Italian way of life.

On the streets, if you are walking with your children, do not be surprised if a man or woman passing by pats a child on the head and says *bel bambino* (pretty boy). Italians are fond of children, both their own and others. The best thing to do when this happens is to say *grazie* (thank you) and smile.

HOSPITALITY

Hospitality in Italy is more than a polite gesture. It is a way of life.

No matter what Italian friends have, they will offer to share it with those around.

The simplest meal of bread, some fruit and wine will be offered to all.

When you start being invited to homes of Italian families, you will discover that every meal is a festive event. The love of conversation comes right to the table along with every member of the family. Good food, accented with some of the country's fine wines, is considered to be one of life's greatest pleasures.

Their hospitality will become even more festive if you have an Italian name or background. Italians value their heritage. In many small towns, summer brings with it the *Festivale Deigle Emigranti,* days of celebration when those who have emigrated to Europe and America return for visits with family and friends.

The bonds of the family are very strong in Italy. Home is considered a castle, a center where aunts, cousins, distant relatives and even some "adopted" ones such as U.S. service members gather as frequently as possible to enjoy talk and meals.

Because of this closeness among families, a birth, a marriage or a death means days of happiness, joyfulness or mourning.

A WORD ABOUT TERRORISM

The likelihood of you or your family members being a victim of terrorism is smaller than well-publicized incidents would have you think. But the threat is real, more so in some places than others. Your local command in country will have the latest guidelines on terrorist activities affecting you and your family. With these guidelines and some common-sense approaches—the same ones you use to protect yourself against being a crime victim—you should feel free to enjoy the benefits of your overseas tour.

Enjoying your tour of duty in a foreign country boils down to a few basic tips:

• Stay alert. Look around and notice what's going on. Follow your instincts if you feel uncomfortable about a situation.

• Keep a low profile. Avoid flashing money, engaging in other such activities that might bring attention to yourself.

• Remain unpredictable. Vary your routine so it's difficult for someone to know when you'll be where and what route you'll follow to get there.

• Immediately report any unusual activity that might be related to security to the appropriate authorities on your base or post.

GETTING AROUND

Your own car is a nice thing to have in Italy, but if it is one of the large models, you may find driving more work than fun.

Streets are crowded with cars, carts, motorbikes, scooters of all sizes and people.

On the highways, the blind curve may just hide an over-laden cart from your view until it is too late.

If you do ship a car, you will have to buy third-party liability insurance to meet the Italian requirements for coverage. If you purchase only the minimum coverage, you will not be covered for death or injuries to passengers in your car. Comprehensive and collision coverage are optional, but recommended.

Your ride from the airport on arrival will give you a good idea of the Italian way of driving.

There are few stoplights at intersections; therefore, very few cars stop. This results in a spirited game of give-and-take on the part of the drivers, along with the waving of arms and loud comments.

When you start driving in Italy, you will find that it is a full-time job. You must drive defensively every moment you are on the road.

A few rules of the road are:

- At intersections where there is no traffic control, cars coming in from the right have the right of way.

- Horn blowing is illegal in most cities and will result in a traffic ticket.

- Drunken driving is as serious an offense in Italy as it is in the states.

- Flash your lights to pass or when approaching intersections.

- Any time you are driving, you must have in the vehicle a valid driver's license for Italy, a *trittico* (proof that the car is in Italy legally) and proof of insurance coverage (either a "green card" or an insurance windshield sticker).

- Finally, DRIVE DEFENSIVELY.

If you are involved in an automobile accident, cooperate fully with the Italian authorities. When you return to your installation, report the incident to the security office and, if necessary, the legal office.

Under Italian law you are required to assist anyone injured in a traffic accident, whether you were involved or were just passing by. You may also be required by the police at an accident scene to transport an injured person to the nearest medical facility, even if you were not involved in any way in the accident.

You don't need a car, however, to see Italy.

Around the cities of the nation, buses run frequently and are cheap. Buses are entered at the rear door. There will he a machine or conductor that will sell you a ticket.

Taxis are also available. If you use a taxi, insist that the meter be turned on. Otherwise, find another taxi. Even with the meter turned on, there will be added charges—figured from a chart the driver will have—for additional passengers, the time of day and amount of luggage carried in the cab. In addition to the fare shown on the meter, a tip of 15 percent will be considered a friendly gesture.

Trains are the best way of getting around the countryside. They are fast and easy to use. You buy your ticket at the Station—either first class or second class-and head off for your adventure. There are dining cars on the long runs, or do as your hosts do—jump off at almost any station stop and purchase some fruit, a sandwich and a bottle of something to drink.

Public transportation is modern, efficient and reasonably priced. Metered taxis are inexpensive and usually available at stands. Avoid unmetered taxis. Most major international airlines have service to Rome and Milan. There is daily jet service to the United States and domestic air service between Italy's major cities and islands.

YOU AND THE LAW

In accordance with the NATO Status of Forces Agreement, the United States military authorities generally have the right to exercise criminal jurisdiction *over U.S. military personnel* for offenses arising out of any act or omission that takes place in the performance of official duty or for offenses that the military member commits that are solely against the security or property of the United States or solely against the person or property of another member of the U.S. forces, the civilian component or a dependent.

In all other cases, *U.S. Forces personnel and their dependents may be tried in Italian courts.*

The Status of Forces Agreement does, however, provide certain safeguards designed to protect basic constitutional rights of U.S. forces personnel, civilian component and dependents when tried by Italian courts.

Drug offense laws are strictly enforced in Italy. Individuals involved with drugs who are apprehended can expect involved and costly trial proceedings and lengthy prison sentences if found guilty.

In Italy there are several major types of police organizations. These are:

- *Carabinieri,* an elite nationwide para-military police force.
- Public security police, who operate under the Ministry of Interior.
- *Stradale police,* the equivalent of our state highway police.
- Customs police (*guardia di finanza*), who work on the borders and at ports.
- City traffic police (*vigili urbani*), the traffic enforcement agents.

You should know that if you receive a traffic ticket—which can be issued on the spot or mailed to you at your residence—you must not ignore it. The fine you will pay triples after 15 days from the day it was mailed.

Most tickets must be paid on the spot. This is legal in Italy and must not be thought of as a shakedown attempt. When you pay, the police officer will give you a receipt.

For the more serious traffic violations, however, the fine cannot be paid on the spot. These violations may result in a criminal charge.

If you are called or summoned to appear before an Italian court, you must report such fact to your commanding officer immediately.

If you are stopped on the street, do not resist arrest. Go with the police, give your name, rank and organization and ask that your military installation be notified.

One last word on the law: Military dependents and civilian employees of the military in Italy are required to obtain a sojourner's (*soggiorno*) permit, which is permission to remain in Italy beyond the 90 days usually granted to tourists. The permit is required in addition to a passport for dependents and civilian employees. The installation security office will have the proper forms to make application. Any change of address, arrival or departure of family members or additions to the family must be reported in order to keep the sojourner's permit current and valid.

FIREARMS

All firearms must be registered with the Italian government after your arrival in Italy. Pistols are restricted to no more than a bore of 7.65mm (.30-caliber).

DAILY LIVING

HOUSING

If you live "on the economy" (off-base), you will need ready cash to pay an agent's commission, a two-month rent deposit and advance rental for one month. Locating suitable detached houses is difficult, and the few available are mostly expensive "villas." Modern apartments with one to three bedrooms are found in the suburbs. Some have pools and tennis courts. Larger apartments are scarce. Most of these quarters are unfurnished.

Furnished apartments with adequate furniture are hard to find, but they do exist. "Furnished" usually means completely furnished, even to pictures, linens and dishes. In contrast, unfurnished apartments often lack light fixtures, kitchen and bathroom cabinets and racks and wardrobes and closets. You can buy these locally and sell them on departure. The newest apartments sometimes include these items. Floor coverings are often needed since even furnished apartments seldom have enough rugs for American tastes. Also, the marble or terrazzo floors found in most apartments and villas are cold in winter. Carpets and rugs are expensive; therefore, bring what you have. American curtains rarely fit windows and the French doors found in Italian apartments. Therefore, buy them locally. Sheets and towels are expensive in Italy.

When you go to rent a house or apartment in Italy, you will have the help of your installation's housing referral office. There, specialists will make certain that you receive a fair contract and pay a fair rent.

AMENITIES

Many buildings are poorly heated by American standards. In apartments with central heating—usually steam radiators—the seasonal heating period is a minimum of 120 days (Nov. 15-May 15). Heat is often off in early morning or late evening hours, so you may need a space heater for a few months.

Gas ranges are economical and preferable, since electricity is expensive.

Standard American appliances are difficult to maintain due to the lack of parts and trained repairmen, something you should keep in mind. Transformers for 110 volt American appliances are sold locally at prices comparable to those in the United States and are also available in the exchanges. Although American lamps can be used with 125 volts or 220 volt current, many 110 volt appliances will not run properly on 125 volts. Thus, transformers are usually required for American appliances. American refrigerators, dishwashers, freezers, washers and dryers usually will not run on European 50-cycle current; with 220 volt equipment, transformers are unnecessary. Such appliances are also available locally at high prices and are small by U.S. standards. Small appliances, too, are available locally or at the exchange.

A 220 volt iron is a good investment because the transformer for an American one costs more than the iron itself.

Turntables and tape recorders (unless direct-drive) must be adapted for 50-cycle operation. This can be done in Italy, but there may be a long delay in getting replacement parts. Other motor-driven appliances run well, but some at lower speed. Voltage fluctuates up to 10 percent, which makes voltage stabilizers useful but not required for stereos or televisions.

SHOPPING

While there will be commissaries and other types of stores on American installations, when in Italy do as the Italians do. Shop at local markets for fresh produce of every type, that wonderful Italian bread, and, of course, the country's famous pastas. It's also a good opportunity to practice your Italian and learn more of the country's language.

A useful measurement to know for marketing at the local stores is the *etto,* which is 100 grams or about one-quarter of a U.S. pound.

PETS

For those interested in shipping the family's pet to Italy, there is no problem if you take the necessary steps.

To ship a dog or cat, you must have in your possession two different Bilingual Health Certificate Forms available from the Italian Embassy, 1601 Fuller St., NW, Washington, D.C. 20009, which must be completed by (1) a veterinarian and then certified by the state health officer of the state where the animal lived, (2) a military veterinarian, or (3) a U.S. Department of Agriculture veterinarian. Animals must be vaccinated against rabies not less than 20 days and not more than 11 months prior to the date of issue of the certificate and must be free of clinical signs of disease. The health certificate is valid for 30 days from the date of issue.

In some areas of Italy, especially crowded cities, there are local laws that require a muzzle and leash for dog walking outdoors. When you arrive at your installation, the local security office will have the information for your area.

HOLIDAYS

Italians enjoy not only 12 legal holidays but also saints' day and festivals that are observed in local towns or regions. The legal holidays are:

New Year's Day, Jan. 1
Epiphany, or Twelfth Night, Jan. 6
Easter Sunday, movable
Easter Monday, movable
Liberation Day, movable
May Day, or Labor Day, May 1
Republic Day, June 2
Assumption Day, Aug.15
All Saints' Day, Nov. 1
Victory Day, Nov. 4
Christmas Day, Dec.25, and
St. Stephens Day, Dec.26.

YOU AND METRIC

MONEY

Be as careful with your money in a foreign land as you would be in the middle of an American city.

The basic unit of Italian currency is the *lira* (plural, *lire*). The value of Italy's money "floats" in relation to the U.S. dollar, so the rate of exchange may differ slightly every day. Change your dollars into lire at the finance office or bank on your installation—that's where you will get the best rate of exchange. Do not change dollars for lire on the streets for two good reasons: (1) It is illegal to do so, and (2) you could be short-changed or given counterfeit lire.

Coins—which seem to be always in short supply—are issued in 10, 50, 100 and 200 lire pieces.

Paper money is issued in 500; 1,000; 2,000; 5,000; 10,000; 50,000; and 100,000 lire notes.

Italy uses the standard metric system Some approximate equivalents to American weights and measures are shown below.

Gram = approximately 1/30 ounce
Kilogram = approximately 2.2 lbs.
Metric ton = approximately 2,204 lbs.
Liter = approximately 1.05 quarts
Hectoliter = approximately 22 gallons
Centimeter = approximately 2/5 inch
Meter = approximately 3.28 feet
Kilometer = approximately 5/8 mile
Hectare = approximately 2½ acres

TEMPERATURE

In Italy, as in the rest of Europe and the world, temperatures are figured on the Centigrade or Celsius scale rather than on the Fahrenheit scale that you are familiar with.

To convert from Centigrade to Fahrenheit, you:
- take the Centigrade reading,
- multiply it by 9,
- divide the result by 5, and
- add 32

Some comparisons:

Fahrenheit	Centigrade
212	100 (boiling point)
100	37.8
80	26.7
70	21.1
50	10
32	0 (freezing point)
0	-17.8

SIZES

If you are buying clothing or shoes in an Italian store, your best bet is to try on each article if it is permitted.

The following sizes are for approximate comparisons.

Dresses

Women

American	10	12	14	16	18	20
Italian	38	40	42	44	46	48

Shoes

American	6	7	8	9	10
Italian	37	38	40	41	42

Suits and Overcoats

Men

American	36	38	40	42	44	46
Italian	46	48	50	52	54	56

Shirts

American	15	16	17	18
Italian	38	41	43	45

Shoes

American	6	7	9	10	11
Italian	39	41	43	44	45

LANGUAGE GUIDE

Learning the language of your host country is one of the first steps in getting to know the people. The following phrases will be useful when you first get to Italy. After you are settled in, take classes at the installation education center.

Don't be bashful about using whatever Italian you know. People in the streets are accustomed to being asked questions by foreigners.

Read the "Pronunciation" column as though it were English. Hyphens divide the words into syllables.

English	Italian	Pronunciation
Good morning, Good day	*Buon giorno*	bwohn JOR-no
Good afternoon, Good evening	*Buona sera*	BWO-na SAY-ra
Sir	*Signore*	seen-Yo-ray
Mister	*Signor*	seen-YOR
Madam	*Signora*	seen-YO-rah

English	Italian	Pronunciation
Miss	*Signorina*	seen-yo-REE-nah
How are you?	*Come sta?*	KO-may STA?
I am well	*Sto bene*	STO BAY-nay
Please	*Per favore*	payr fa-VO-ray
Thank you	*Grazie*	GRAHTS-yay
You are welcome	*Prego*	PRAY-go
Excuse me	*Scusi*	SKOO-zee
Do you understand?	*Ha capito?*	ah ka-PEE-to?
I do not understand	*Non capisco*	NOHN ka-pee-sko
Please repeat	*Ripeta, per favore*	ree-PAY-tah, payr fa-VO-ray
Yes	*Si*	SEE
No	*No*	NO
Maybe	*Forse*	FOR-say
What is your name?	*Come Si chiama?*	KO-may see KYAH-mah?
My name is____	*Mi chiama____*	Mee KYAH moh____
Goodby	*Arrivederci*	ar-ree-vay-DAYR-chee

GETTING AROUND

Where is____?	*Dov' è____?*	DOH-vay____?
hotel	*Un albergo*	oon ahl-BAYR-go
a restaurant	*on ristorante*	oon ree-sto-RAHN-tay
This way?	*Da questa parte?*	do KWESS-ta PAR-tay
That way?	*Da quella parte?*	da KWEL-la PAR-tay

31

English	Italian	Pronunciation
Which is the road to _____?	*Qual'è la strada per_____?*	kwah-LAY lah STRAHdah payr _____?
Kilometer(s)	*Chilometro/ Chilometri*	kee-LO-met-ro/ kee-LO-met-ree

ASKING FOR THINGS

What is this?	*Che cosa è questo?*	kay KOH-zah eh KWESS-to?
What is that?	*Che cosa è quello?*	kay KOH-zah eh KWEL-lo?
How much?	*Quanto?*	KWAHN-to?
I want	*Voglio_____*	VOHL-yo_____
coffee	*del caffè*	del kahf-FAY
wine	*del vino*	del VEE-no
food	*da mangiare*	da mahn-JA-ray
The check, please	*Il conto, per favore*	eel KON-to, payr-fa-VO-ray
I want a taxi	*Voglio un tassi*	VOHL-yo ooa tass-SEE

DAYS AND MONTHS

Yesterday	*Ieri*	ee-EH-ree
Today	*Oggi*	AWjee
Tomorrow	*Domani*	doh-MAH-nee
Sunday	*Domenica*	dob-MAY-nee-kab
Monday	*Lunedi*	loo-nay-DEE
Tuesday	*Martedi*	mahr-tay-DEE
Wednesday	*Mercoledi*	mayr-koh-lay-DEE
Thursday	*Giovedi*	joh-vay-DEE
Friday	*Venerdi*	vay-nayr-DEE
Saturday	*Sabato*	SAH-bab-toh

English	Italian	Pronunciation
January	*Gennaio*	ja-NAH-yoh
February	*Febbraio*	fay-BRAH-yoh
March	*Marzo*	Mar-tzoh
April	*Aprile*	ah-PREE-lay
May	*Maggio*	MAH-joh
June	*Giugno*	JOON-yoh
July	*Luglio*	LOOL-yoh
August	*Argots*	ah-GOH-stoh
September	*Settembre*	say-TEM-bray
October	*Ottobre*	oh-TOH-bray
November	*Novembre*	noh-VEM-bray
December	*Dicembre*	dee-CHEM-bray

NUMBERS

one	*uno*	OO-noh
two	*due*	DOO-ay
three	*tre*	TRAY
four	*quattro*	KWAHT-troh
five	*cinque*	CHEEN-kway
six	*sei*	SAY
seven	*sette*	SET-tay
eight	*otto*	AW-toh
nine	*nove*	NAW-vay
ten	*diece*	DYAY-chee

SIGNS FREQUENTLY SEEN

Italian	English
Alt!	Stop!
Pericolo	Danger
Attenzione	Caution
Rallentare!	Go slow!
Deviazione	Detour
Svolta pericolosa	Dangerous curve
Vietato il transito	No thoroughfare
Strada chiusa	Dead end
Tenere la destra	Keep to the right
Senso unico	One way
Divieto di parcheggio	No parking
Entrata	Entrance
Uscita	Exit
E proibito avvicinarsi	Keep out
Ritirata	Lavatory
Signore or Donne	Women
Signori or Uomini	Men
Aperto	Open
Chiuso	Closed

SIGHTS TO SEE

There are too many places to visit and things to see to be covered in this small brochure.

However, the American armed forces have been in Italy for years. Every installation library has a special section set aside for the books on Italy—things to see and do in the area of the installation as well as throughout the country. Education centers offer evening courses so you can learn to speak Italian.

The opportunities to enjoy Italy are there, if you make the first move.

It would be sad, indeed, if you lived for several years in Italy and never:

- Saw the temples, statues and the colosseum of the ancient Roman Empire preserved amidst the hustle and bustle of Rome, the nation's capital;
- Heard an opera in Verona or Milan;
- Visited the Vatican, center of the Roman Catholic

Church and home of the pope; or

• Enjoyed the art works displayed in large museums and country churches.

Your service club and local travel agencies can send you off on tours for a weekend, a week or a month.

The sights and sounds of this fascinating land and the friendliness of the people will be cherished memories for the rest of your life.

Food—good food—is a way of living for all Italians. They enjoy eating, the company of the table and having the time to savor the various dishes. Once you get settled in and become familiar with the language, head out for a meal on the town.

Restaurants come in many types and sizes.

Some, like the stand-up bars that serve breakfast, offer a roll and a *cappucino*, coffee topped with a froth of steamed milk.

Others will be more familiar to Americans. The *tavola calda*—hot table—restaurant will offer a variety of hot dishes but not full meals. You go along the table, take your pick and pay at the other end.

A different dining experience awaits you at one of the countless *trattorias*—neighborhood restaurants. You'll find an empty seat, get the day's menu from the friendly waiter—probably with a lot of help from your neighboring diners if you're having difficulty understanding the bill of fare—and enjoy a tasty, filling meal. A glass of the local wine is a suitable addition to the meal.

Then, there are the full restaurants. Because so many

tourists visit Italy every year, many restaurants of this type are required to offer a tourist menu. It will be posted outside in four languages.

If you want to strike out on your own, try the regular menu.

Regional specialties will be offered in the larger restaurants along with just about every type of food that you are familiar with from the United States.

Try starting a meal with an *antipasto*. This can be just about anything and is offered to whet the appetite.

Then comes the soup course, followed by a *pasta* course.

These are followed by the entree, a meat or fish course. Vegetables are served as an extra dish.

Salad usually follows the entree to freshen the mouth. Then, if you still have room, you have a choice of cheese or fruit, some kind of dessert and your *expresso*—Italy's gift to the coffee drinkers of the world.

GETTING READY TO GO

Going on a tour of duty in Italy is no different than any trip. It may take a little more preparation, but if you start preparing early, you should have no difficulties.

As a member of the U.S. armed forces, all you need to enter Italy on your tour are official military orders and your armed forces identification card. These same documents can be used as identification on your travels about the country.

Dependents of service members must have both current United States passports and dependents' military identification cards. It is recommended by the Department of State that every member of the family have his or her own passport. This will allow flexibility in independent vacation travel and for emergency leave. Military identification cards should be obtained for every dependent over 10 years of age.

Another important document for every family member is a current immunization record. Your local military medical facility will have a list of immunization requirements.

Special medical care needs for any member of the family should be reported to the appropriate authorities in your service as soon as you receive your orders.

Since express shipments can be delayed, it makes good sense to carry certain items with you as you travel to Italy. Here's a basic list of things you will need on the trip and for the first days after your arrival.

CHECKLIST

Personal Items

- Passport—one for the sponsor and one for each family member
- Military identification cards for every family member
- Permanent change of station orders—at least three copies for sponsor and each family member
- Immunization record—complete record for every family member, plus copies of other vital health records. If any member of the family needs special health care, that fact should be reported to your service health authorities as soon as PCS orders are received
- Current driver's license for every adult member
- School records for each child, including last report cards
- Birth certificates for all members; adoption papers (if any)
- Marriage certificate(s); divorce/annulment decree(s)
- Power of attorney, if needed
- Copy of current will and letter of instruction
- Copies of prescriptions for every family member

- Naturalization document(s), if any
- Uniforms, civilian clothing as required

POV, Household

- Vehicle title, registration
- Extra set of car keys
- Insurance policies on POV, household goods. family members
- Inventory of household goods being shipped
- Measurements of furniture, appliances shipped

For Travel

- Overnight toilet articles, including toilet paper
- Portable radio, battery operated
- Traveler's checks, other forms of funds
- U.S. bank checkbook, extra checks
- Portcall instructions
- One-cup heating element, 110/230v
- Alarm clock, windup model

Other Items

- Credit cards, with list of numbers and addresses where to report loss
- List of companies due payment from you, with addresses
- Safe deposit box key. with list of items in box
- Previous discharge certificate, if any
- High school, college records
- Information from the installation veterinarian office if pet is to be shipped

THE SECRETARY OF DEFENSE
Washington, D.C.
July 1987

July 1987

A POCKET GUIDE TO ITALY (DoD PG-6B)—This official Department of Defense publication is for the use of personnel in the military services.